Santa's Little Instruction Book

Have You Been Naughty or Nice?

Scott Matthews and Barbara Alpert

PINNACLE BOOKS

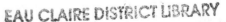

PINNACLE BOOKS are published by

Windsor Publishing Corp.
850 Third Ave
New York, NY 10022

First Printing: December, 1994

Printed in the United States of America

To my North Star, my wife, Tamara Nikuradse
—S.M.

For my parents, who taught me to celebrate life.
—B.A.

1. Don't be a Scrooge.

2. Deck the halls.

3. Bring joy to the world.

4. Don't tie jingle bells to the dog's tail.

5. Find the North Star in the night sky, and remember how the Wise Men found their way.

6. Encourage the dreams of those you love.

7. Bring your pets to church to be blessed.

8. Be a peacemaker—in your family, your town, your school.

9. Learn all of Santa's reindeers' names.

10. Count your blessings.

11. Make a Christmas angel in the snow.

12. Practice kindness.

13. Keep a twinkle in your eye.

14. When people tell you something's impossible, prove them wrong.

15. Join with others to make your neighborhood glow.

16. It's not size but thoughtfulness that counts when buying gifts.

17. Remember the spirit of Tiny Tim.

18. Give a tiny potted pine tree for a child's first Christmas. By the time he or she leaves for college, it will have grown tall.

19. Don't gossip; share only good news.

20. Listen to your angels . . . and the little voice inside that gives you hope.

21. Never take what isn't yours. Ask to borrow it.

22. Feel the wonder of a midnight clear.

23. Give sleighs the right of way.

24. Love yourself as you are.

25. Clean the chimney before Christmas Eve.

26. Dream of sugar plums.

27. Don't pack your snowballs too hard.

28. Keep a candle burning in your window.

29. Help pull off everybody's snow boots.

30. Treasure friendships, and stay in touch.

31. Start a new tradition, and cherish the ones you have.

32. Send a "just because I love you" note to someone you miss.

33. Share your home for the holidays.

34. Wrap an extra present to donate to Toys for Tots.

35. Heal a broken heart.

36. Watch *It's a Wonderful Life* with the sound turned off, and see who can remember all the dialogue.

37. Lead Christmas caroling at a home for the elderly.

38. Remember to say please and thank you.

39. Confront your ghosts of Christmases past.

40. Be Santa's little helper.

41. Don't be an abominable snowman.

42. Invite your favorite elf to share a bubble bath.

43. Never turn off the radio when someone's singing a carol.

44. Let it snow.

45. Don't climb down the chimney—that's Santa's job.

46. Button up your overcoat.

47. Keep a pair of snowshoes handy for emergency rescues.

48. If you're home alone for the holidays, invite a friend over.

49. Wear your galoshes.

50. Make time between Bowl games for your family.

51. Persevere like Rudolph.

52. Help a child send a letter to the North Pole.

53. Wrap tiny presents in huge boxes.

54. Keep Jack Frost from nipping by wearing thermal socks.

55. Calories don't count on Christmas Day.

56. Be a volunteer Santa at a kids' Christmas party.

57. Take turns carving the turkey.

58. Fall asleep to the crackling of a fire.

59. Find an extra-long toboggan so the family can ride together.

60. Build a Dream Team of snowmen.

61. Make costumes for the school Christmas pageant.

62. Don't lick icy flagpoles even if you're dared.

63. Drop gentle hints about what you'd like for Christmas.

64. Climb a snow-covered hill just because it's there.

65. Instead of a snow fort, build an igloo.

66. When your lips turn blue, it's time to go inside.

67. Answer your phone with a "Ho-Ho-Ho!"

68. Rejoice.

69. Leave the "Bah humbugs" to Scrooge.

70. Serve visiting carolers hot chocolate with real milk.

71. Keep the TV off on Christmas Day.

72. Spread the Good News.

73. Treasure all the gifts you receive.

74. Don't decorate your office like the mall at Christmas.

75. Start writing New Year's resolutions now.

76. Remind yourself it's better to give than receive.

77. Reunite with childhood friends to celebrate your memories.

78. Don't rain on anyone's parade.

79. Remember, the sun's behind the clouds.

80. Relish the pleasure of watching someone open your gift.

81. Try to find two snowflakes that look alike.

82. Carry a friend's sled up the hill.

83. Make a bed for your pets beside the fireplace.

84. Dress in holiday style.

85. Make peace with your parents.

86. Keep your own Christmas vigil.

87. Enjoy the beauty of fresh fallen snow.

88. Breathe deeply on cold, crisp days.

89. Fill your bird feeder to overflowing when the weather is coldest.

90. Trim your tree to the tune of "O, Tannenbaum."

91. Be worthy of trust.

92. Defend those who can't defend themselves.

93. Spoil your grandparents.

94. Be jolly.

95. Sing along to the Yule Log burning on TV.

96. Hang mistletoe over your bed.

97. Make merry.

98. Grant three wishes.

99. String cranberries to hang on the tree.

100. Don't be a critic.

101. Wear tinsel in your hair.

102. Make an exception to the rule.

103. Surround yourself with pictures of your loved ones.

104. Plan now for the future.

105. Know when to stop.

106. Believe in your right to be loved.

107. Go looking for a wise man or two.

108. Shine like the brightest star in the heavens.

109. Aim your hopes high.

110. Don't put coal in anyone's stocking.

111. Catch a snowflake with your tongue.

112. Hug a child every day. (If you don't have kids of your own, borrow a friend's.)

113. Be a child again . . . and revel in the spirit of the season.

114. Don't drive your parents nuts.

115. You can never have too much self-esteem.

116. Learn to use the timer on your camera so everyone can be in all the pictures.

117. Bring tidings of comfort and joy.

118. Keep your temper.

119. Be a fool for love.

120. Make a child giggle with a goofy joke.

121. Better to be safe than sorry.

122. Turn every trip into an adventure.

123. Wear red underwear.

124. Believe in magic.

125. Dip apples in caramel for a sweet New Year.

126. Go running through a forest of evergreens.

127. Let people exceed your expectations.

128. Free your imagination.

129. Learn from your children.

130. Have a real tree this year.

131. Admit it when you're wrong.

132. Hang bells on your front door.

133. Believe the best is yet to come.

134. Ask for help when you need it.

135. Watch the National Christmas Tree lighting at the White House.

136. Emulate your parents.

137. Make gingerbread people to give as gifts.

138. Lick the cleanest icicle you can find.

139. Express your love.

140. Teach a child to make paper chains
for the tree.

141. Never quit.

142. Wear a sprig of mistletoe and keep your lips puckered.

143. Don't try to be perfect, but do your best.

144. Volunteer at a children's hospital or soup kitchen.

145. Have faith.

146. Sing loud.

147. Hug tight.

148. Be tender.

149. Call when you say you will.

150. Cherish the people who matter the most.

151. Think of those you loved who passed on during this year—and give the gift of remembrance.

152. Make your own fruitcake.

153. Be happy—it's the best gift you can give to the people who love you.

154. Pile up enough fireplace logs to burn all December long.

155. Fly high and land gently.

156. Tell your parents you love them.

157. Don't forget to watch the sunset even when the days are short.

158. Go to church on Christmas Day.

159. Wear pajamas with feet in them.

160. Pray for peace.

161. Celebrate the shortest day of the year.

162. Dream all through the longest night.

163. Imagine each star is the spirit of someone you loved.

164. Learn to make origami cranes to decorate the tree.

165. Roll around in a snowdrift.

166. Make a new friend.

167. Never burn your bridges.

168. Write "I love you" on a frosty window.

169. Don't stand under icicles.

170. Light a candle to help you find your way.

171. Ask a friend to help you tie perfect bows.

172. Pin a sprig of holly to your lapel.

173. Give your heart.

174. Practice blowing "smoke" rings with your icy breath.

175. Laugh until you shake like a bowl full of jelly.

176. Warm your hands before touching someone.

177. Give good will.

178. Give to Goodwill.

179. Share your luck with others.

180. Heal the world with your spirit.

181. Put hatred from your heart.

182. Enchant a child with the story of Christmas.

183. Give your love a Christmas rose.

184. Eat mince pie without reading the ingredients.

185. Share what you have.

186. Settle a quarrel beneath a branch of holly.

187. Drink a toast to the health of everyone present.

188. Listen for the sound of trumpets.

189. Reach out to the lonely.

190. Ask forgiveness.

191. Always keep a pot of mulled cider on the stove.

192. Pin your mittens to your coat sleeves.

193. Let your brother use the bathroom first.

194. Name your goldfish "Holly."

195. Laugh all the way.

196. Make homemade gifts.

197. Dash through the snow.

198. Add another strand of lights to the tree.

199. Be considerate.

200. Invite your in-laws to share your Christmas.

201. Make spirits bright.

202. Have a child's sense of wonder.

203. Do what you love—love what you do.

204. Tuck your children all snug in their beds.

205. If you're driving, skip the spiked eggnog.

206. Make someone happy.

207. Laugh out loud.

208. Give the greatest gift of all—yourself.

209. Make a salt lick for the deer.

210. Give a newly married couple a special ornament to mark their first Christmas together.

211. Practice infinite understanding.

212. Let your light shine.

213. Be generous with your affection, and stingy with your anger.

214. Follow your heart to a place beyond your limits.

215. Thank God for unanswered prayers.

216. Lift the littlest child in the room to place the angel or star on the top of your tree.

217. Forgive and forget.

218. Practice Christmas carols in the shower.

219. Keep secrets.

220. Call your mother and share memories of the best Christmases you ever had.

221. Ask your father to tell you about his favorite Christmas morning as a boy.

222. Always wear your seatbelt.

223. Be proud of yourself.

224. Practice gratitude for the people you treasure and the good health you enjoy.

225. Never lose your sense of humor.

226. Tape record your grandparents when they speak of their childhood and family.

227. Be someone's hero.

228. Make your days merry and bright.

229. Listen to your own advice.

230. Don't pout.

231. Kiss and rub noses like the "Eskimoses."

232. Know what you know.

233. Make love contagious—spread it around.

234. Listen to the silent night.

235. Let the people you love hear you compliment them.

236. Shovel the previous night's snowfall from your neighbors' walk and driveway before they wake up.

237. Stay open to possibilities.

238. Invite a child to bake and decorate holiday cookies.

239. Seize the day.

240. Believe in miracles.

241. Take the road less traveled.

242. Make someone's Christmas wish come true.

243. Be yourself.

244. Appreciate the little things.

245. Put your love in writing.

246. Ring a bell from time to time—and help an angel get her wings.

247. Be good for goodness' sake.

248. Empty your closets of clothing you no longer wear, and give it to the Salvation Army.

249. Be patient.

250. Learn something new this month, and practice it every day.

251. Turn the television off for a full 24 hours, and listen to holiday music instead.

252. Call your friends and family.

253. Love more, worry less, and keep your heart open.

254. Celebrate the good times.

255. Say your prayers before you go to sleep.

256. Bring a basket of holiday foods to a needy family.

257. Rescue a kitten from the animal shelter. Name her "Prancer."

258. Listen for the prayers of children.

259. Don't pick on your siblings, even if they're driving you crazy.

260. Tell your mother that she looks beautiful.

261. Be thoughtful.

262. Ask why.

263. Write your own Christmas story and read it to a group of children.

264. Be the first to blaze a trail through the snow.

265. Don't hurt anyone's feelings.

266. Bake Christmas cookies for the homeless.

267. Celebrate the differences in people.

268. Wish upon a star.

269. Find the courage to chase your dreams.

270. Put all your toys away where they belong.

271. Don't forget that Christmas is a birthday party, after all.

272. Use your failures as stepping-stones.

273. Do a brave deed.

274. Be a vixen—wear a hat with antlers.

275. Forgive yourself.

276. Read " 'Twas the Night Before Christmas" aloud.

277. Regret as little as possible.

278. Share a sleigh ride with a loved one and hold on tight.

279. Don't lie. (Little fibs are okay if you're
      trying to throw people off the trail when
      they're guessing their Christmas gifts.)

280. Spread your wings.

281. Make more time for your family and loved
      ones.

282. Hang a Christmas stocking filled with squeaky toys and treats for your favorite pet.

283. Let peace begin with you.

284. Do your chores without being asked.

285. Don't let the Grinch steal your Christmas.

286. Notice everyday miracles.

287. Be generous with tips and smiles.

288. Be an angel.

289. Put your troubles behind you.

290. Be spontaneous.

291. Baby-sit for a friend who needs a night out.

292. Be a secret Santa—and fulfill a heart's desire.

293. Offer to jump-start a stranded motorist.

294. Buy an Advent calendar, and count down the days until Christmas.

295. Keep hope alive.

296. Be nice to overworked sales clerks. It's their holiday, too.

297. Start small and keep going.

298. Rest on the Sabbath.

299. Leave a light on for Santa.

300. Watch the sky for shooting stars.

301. Be curious.

302. Organize a group of friends to go Christmas caroling at a hospital or nursing home.

303. Listen more. Talk less.

304. Deliver on your promises.

305. Eat Christmas cookies in bed.

306. Learn from your mistakes.

307. Volunteer for holiday storytelling duty.

308. Tell that special someone, "You're my one and only."

309. Don't skate on thin ice.

310. Use your common sense.

311. Don't peek at your gifts under the Christmas tree.

312. Let your dreams exceed your grasp.

313. Be nice to chubby men in red suits and beards.

314. Make your own luck.

315. Attend Midnight Mass.

316. Reread old love letters and remember the wonder.

317. Give the best back rub you know how, and hope for a good one in return.

318. Remember, the best gifts are free.

319. Save the planet for our children.

320. Be nourished by the long roots in your family tree.

321. Accept the advice of well-meaning friends.

322. Drop your spare change in the charity kettles.

323. Send a Christmas card to a teacher who changed your life.

324. Donate your canned goods to people in need.

325. Gather your family around you to watch for the first evening star.

326. Find out which of your friends are ticklish.

327. Add a new ornament to the tree to celebrate each new family member.

328. Walk the dog, even if it's not your turn.

329. Trust your instincts.

330. Carry the Christmas spirit with you 365 days of the year.

331. Reach for the stars.

332. Smile at yourself every time you look in the mirror.

333. Don't try to be Martha Stewart.

334. Tell your biggest fans how much their support means.

335. Leave your wet boots on the mat.

336. Count to ten when you get mad. Then count to 100, just to be sure.

337. Don't stick your finger where it doesn't belong.

338. Change the world for the better.

339. Don't eat candy canes off the tree.

340. Dream of a white Christmas—just like the ones you used to know.

341. Don't stuff your kitten in a stocking.

342. When opportunity knocks, open the door.

343. Stop at the next Nativity scene that you come across and marvel at the meaning of the age-old story.

344. Bounce back even higher when you stumble and fall.

345. Don't waste your time being jealous.

346. Seek knowledge that casts light on the path you plan to follow.

347. Wish Christ a happy birthday.

348. Treasure your memories.

349. If your family can't get home for
Christmas, celebrate anytime, anywhere.

350. Leave skim milk and sugar-free cookies for
Santa. The reindeer will be grateful.

351. Master your fears.

352. Try to do your Christmas shopping before Thanksgiving.

353. Praise your kids.

354. Watch for reindeer running amok when you cross the street.

355. Make your own Christmas cards.

356. Don't throw away the cat with the gift wrapping.

357. Remember to shop for half-price ornaments and cards right after Christmas.

358. Visit the zoo and wish the reindeer Merry Christmas.

359. To discover new oceans, you have to lose sight of the shore.

360. Give up guilt.

361. Make your home a sanctuary.

362. If you haven't gone to church in a long time, Christmas is a good time to find your faith again.

363. Don't wait until it's too late to realize you've had a wonderful life.

364. Let this season of joyous birth signal a new beginning for you, too.

365. Have a very merry Christmas.

MY WISH LIST FOR SANTA

1. _____
2. _____
3. _____
4. _____
5. _____
6. _____
7. _____
8. _____
9. _____
10. _____

May all your Christmas wishes come true.

Scott Matthews is a publishing executive who lives with his wife and three cats in New York City. He is also co-author of *Dear Mom/Dad: Thank You for Being Mine*, *To the Man/Woman I Love: Thank You for Being Mine*, and *Stuck in the Seventies*.

Barbara Alpert is a book editor and writer who's published short fiction and nonfiction in national magazines. When she's not traveling to Tanzania or Antarctica photographing wildlife, she shares a New York City apartment with two cats.